Obamacare Survival Guide: Beating Obamacare and the New HealthCare Law

Betty Macroal

All Rights Reserved. No part of this publication may be reproduced in any form or by any means, including scanning, photocopying, or otherwise without prior written permission of the copyright holder.

Copyright Jaba Publishing© 2013

This guide is meant to be a general representation of the laws currently in effect. No legal or financial guidance is given. You should talk with a professional account and tax adviser about your unique situation.

The Patient Protection and Affordable Care Act, more commonly known as Obamacare, is the most significant overhaul to the health care industry in decades. It includes unprecedented legal reforms affecting the American health care system. The implementation of this new health care law, is at the height of concern for many who still don't understand its implications. Among the sea of new information to sift through, there are also misconceptions about the expectations and implementations of this law.

Whether you need health insurance coverage or have it already you may be concerned about the new regulations and how they will affect you. Many low to middle income Americans will now have access to more affordable health insurance but those making above 400% of the federal poverty will likely pay more.

Although the law has been rolled out over several years, the most notable changes take effect in January of 2014. Included in these changes are new rights and protections for you, the consumer. These protections do not apply to every insurance policy equally.

This guide is designed to help you navigate the changes in policies and the new requirements for individuals and businesses. We'll explain the changes being implemented and you'll discover if you qualify for reduced premiums, what will happen if you select not to purchase health care, and how to compare plans and policies in your state.

The Basics of Health Insurance

Health insurance has a lot of associated jargon. Understanding the basics will help you navigate the new health care law and its implications.

Health insurance is designed to protect your wallet from burdensome medical costs. It does not pay for all of your medical costs because you share them. People without health coverage are responsible for all of their medical payments and many have been lead into deep debt and eventual bankruptcy.

When you purchase a health insurance plan, you pay a monthly fee. This is called a <u>premium</u>. You pay your premium every month even if the insurance company does not pay any medical bills on your behalf. If you purchase health insurance at work, your employer may pay a portion of your premium on your behalf.

When you go to the doctor's office, you will often need to make a payment called a <u>copayment</u>. This payment is usually less than it would cost if you did not have insurance, and the insurance company will pay the difference. You may have a different copayment due for different types of medical services. For example, you may pay a $25 copayment to see your general physician and a $50 copayment to see a specialist.

If your doctor orders tests or x-rays, you will need to pay for those services (and the health insurance company will not make a payment) until you have met your <u>deductible</u>. The size of your deductible will vary based on your plan and types of service. Typically, the more you pay in monthly premiums, the lower your deductible will be.

Although you pay a deductible for many services, your health insurance company may pay for preventive services such as well-care exams even if you have not met your deductible. You will also likely pay less than you would have if you did not have insurance because insurance companies have negotiated lower rates for their policy holders.

After you have met your deductible, your insurance plan will begin to pay some of your medical costs. You will still be responsible for a portion. The portion you are responsible for is called <u>coinsurance</u>. Your coinsurance is usually a percentage of your health insurance bill. The higher your monthly premium, the lower your coinsurance is likely to be. Your coinsurance obligations end when your annual <u>out of pocket maximum</u> has been reached.

An out of pocket maximum is the total amount you will pay in one calendar year for health insurance services. This maximum does not include the amount you pay in premiums and many times it does not include the amount you have paid in copayments.

Getting Health Insurance

If you do not have coverage that meets the <u>minimum essential coverage</u> standards, starting in January 2014, you may have to pay a <u>fee.</u> You will also be responsible for 100% of your health care costs.

The Affordable Care act does not require you to purchase specific policies, but it does offer policies through a marketplace which makes it easy for the consumer to compare prices and plans with or without the help of an insurance agent. If you qualify for a reduction in premiums or out of pocket costs, those reductions will only be applied to certain plans within the marketplace.

There are several ways you can purchase a health insurance policy. You can purchase a health insurance policy through your employer if they offer it. Your employer may contribute to your premiums thereby reducing your monthly cost. You can also purchase a policy through an agent or directly through an insurance company. Finally, you can purchase a health insurance plan directly through the health insurance marketplace.

If you want to purchase a policy though the marketplace you can pick a plan on your mobile phone or call 1-800-318-2596 and a Customer Service Representative will help you. TTY users can call 1-855-889-4325.

The best way to apply online for coverage, compare plans, and enroll is to visit HealthCare.gov on a desktop or laptop computer. You can also look at the plan finder. The plan finder lists policies available to you in your area but should not be confused with the healthcare Marketplace.

If you can't afford a health plan, you may be able to get low-cost health care at a nearby community health center. The amount you pay for services at a community health center depends on your income. These centers typically provide:

- prenatal care
- baby shots

- general primary care

- referrals to specialized care

Locate a community health center near you.

Other Health Insurance Options

Based on your income, you may qualify for any of the following:

Medicaid provides coverage to millions of Americans with limited incomes or disabilities. Each state's Medicaid rules are different. Many states are expanding Medicaid in 2014 to cover more people. You can apply for Medicaid in your state now to see if you are eligible. Or you can fill out a Marketplace application to find out if you will qualify in your state in 2014.

Children's Health Insurance Program (CHIP) provides coverage for children, and sometimes pregnant women whose families have incomes too high for Medicaid but too low to afford private insurance. When you fill out a Marketplace application, you will be screened to find out if you're eligible for CHIP.

Lower costs on <u>Marketplace</u> insurance. You may qualify for reduced monthly premiums and lower out-of-pocket costs on health insurance listed in the marketplace. Savings are based on your household size and income. It is expected that most people who apply for insurance though the Marketplace will receive some sort of savings.

Find local help

In all states, there are people trained and certified to help you understand your health insurance options and assist you in enrolling in a plan. They have different names, depending on where they are located.

- Navigators
- Application assistance
- Certified application counselors
- Government agencies, such as State Medicaid and Children's Health Insurance Program (CHIP) Offices

Insurance agents and brokers can also help you with your application and choices.

Visit LocalHelp.HealthCare.gov to find help in your area. You can search by city and state or zip code to see a list of local organizations with contact information, office hours, and types of help offered, such as non-English language support, Medicaid or CHIP, and Small Business Health Options Program (SHOP).

Get help with your application online

The Marketplace website walks you step-by-step through the online health coverage application. Pay attention to each page as it explains how much time each step might take and if you'll need any forms or documents to complete. If you want live help while you apply, you can call the toll-free support center or chat with someone online.

How much is this going to cost?

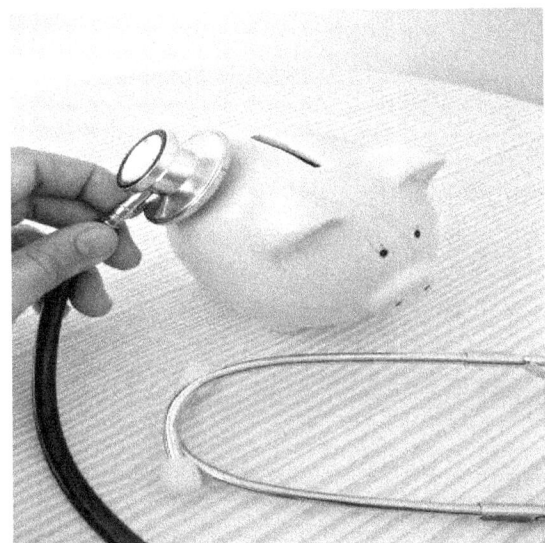

If you already have an insurance policy through work or an individual insurance plan that meets the minimum coverage requirements, you are not required to make any changes. In order to view the plans in the Health Insurance Marketplace, you'll need to complete an application. As part of the application process, you'll provide information about your household size and income which will help determine if you qualify for **lower costs on your monthly premiums** or lower out of pocket costs. The Marketplace will also help determine if you qualify for free or low-cost coverage available through Medicaid or the Children's Health Insurance Program (CHIP).

If you want to learn more about your options without completing an application, you can use the Keiser family cost and savings calculator or preview plans and prices. The calculator gives you a rough estimate of what insurance might cost you based on where you live, the age and size of your family, and if you use tobacco. The premiums displayed by the calculator are only estimates and only give you an idea of what someone in your area and age might pay for an individual health insurance plan in the Silver category. The premiums displayed on the preview page do not reflect any savings for which you may qualify.

You can use a different tool to see plans and sample prices available in your area. This tool shows specific plans and sample prices, but it does not account for any savings you may qualify for based on your income. The only way to get a specific and accurate price is to complete a Marketplace application. The sample prices are what someone would pay if they did not qualify for savings.

Deductibles, copayments, and other out-of-pocket costs are omitted from the search results. More information on specific plans are available after you complete the application in the Marketplace.

If you are serious about knowing your health insurance options, then it is worth spending a few minutes to complete an application. You will not be able to know your exact premiums and if you qualify for reductions in cost until you complete an application.

Qualifying for Marketplace savings

Your income may qualify you for lower premiums if your employer does not offer health insurance coverage. If your employer does offer coverage but it does not offer the minimum benefits, or it the coverage is not considered affordable, you may qualify for lower premiums. You won't qualify for lower costs if your job-based coverage is considered affordable and meets minimum value.

Your employer based health plan is considered affordable if your share of the premium (for you not your family) is 9.5% of your income or less. Percentages are based on annual premiums and annual salaries.

The total you pay in insurance premiums may exceed 9.5% of your income when they include coverage for your family members, but this does not make the coverage unaffordable.

Joe pays $500 of insurance premiums every month ($6000 a year) through his employer based health plan. He earns $60000 a year. Joe's premiums are 10% of his annual income.

If Joe is only purchasing coverage for himself, then his employer based plan is not considered affordable and Joe might qualify for reduced premiums on a plan listed within the marketplace plan. If Joe is purchasing coverage for his wife and himself, only the portion he is paying for his own coverage is considered when determining if the plan is affordable.

3 ways to save on health care coverage

One of the benefits of getting health insurance coverage with a plan listed in the marketplace is you may be able to get lower monthly premiums, out-of-pocket costs, or get free or low-cost coverage.

Depending on your household size and income, you may be able to save money 3 different ways. You may qualify for lower premiums, lower out of pocket costs (through smaller copayments and deductibles) or you may qualify for free and/or low-cost coverage with Medicaid or Chip.

Out-of-pocket savings only apply to Silver plans

If you qualify for out-of-pocket savings, you must choose a Silver plan to get them. The out-of-pocket savings offer the benefits of a Gold or Platinum plan at a Silver plan price. You can choose any category of plan, but you'll get the out-of-pocket savings only if you enroll in a Silver plan.

The difference between plans

The health insurance plans listed in the Marketplace are called qualified health plans. They provide a minimum set of benefits, features, and protections. Health insurance plans available outside the Marketplace often offer the same minimums however the only way to receive premium reductions or reduced out of pocket costs, is to purchase a plan within the Marketplace.

If you want a plan outside the Marketplace

You can also choose to get coverage outside the Marketplace. You will have up to 30 days after your plan ends to sign up for a new plan outside the Marketplace. You may not be able to buy or change health plans inside or outside the Marketplace outside of the open enrollment period. Qualifying life events like marriage, birth of a child, or loss of other health coverage will allow you to purchase a policy outside of the open enrollment period.

Individuals making less than $45,000 a year and or families of 4 earning less than $94,000, may qualify for some price reductions. In the Health Insurance Marketplace you may be able to lower the costs of your health insurance coverage by paying lower monthly premiums. You'll see the amount of savings you're eligible for when you fill out your Marketplace application. Prices shown for insurance plans will reflect the lower costs.

The lower costs are provided with and advance premium with a tax credit which is applied directly to your monthly premiums. If your income and family size fall within the ranges below, you will likely qualify for a reduction in premiums.

$11,490 to $45,960 for individuals
$15,510 to $62,040 for a family of 2
$19,530 to $78,120 for a family of 3
$23,550 to $94,200 for a family of 4
$27,570 to $110,280 for a family of 5
$31,590 to $126,360 for a family of 6
$35,610 to $142,440 for a family of 7
$39,630 to $158,520 for a family of 8

If your income falls above or below the ranges above, you will not qualify for premium reductions. You may, however, qualify for Medicaid. By completing an application, you will learn which programs and discounts for which you qualify.

In order to receive lower out of pockets costs you'll need to fall in the income range below. (Based on the year 2013)

- Up to $28,725 for individuals
- Up to $38,775 for a family of 2
- Up to $48,825 for a family of 3
- Up to $58,875 for a family of 4
- Up to $68,925 for a family of 5
- Up to $78,975 for a family of 6
- Up to $89,025 for a family of 7
- Up to $99,075 for a family of 8

How to determine your family size:

When completing your application, include yourself, your spouse, the children who live with you, anyone you include on a tax return as a dependent and your unmarried partner (if they need health insurance coverage.) You should not include an unmarried partner if they do not need health insurance or your partner's children if they are not your dependents.

You can learn about who qualifies as a dependent in IRS Publication 501.

Mixed status families

Many immigrant families are of "mixed status," with members having different immigration and citizenship statuses. The same situation could apply in a family that has some members who are not eligible for full Medicaid, and others who are eligible for Medicaid or CHIP.

"Mixed status" families can apply for a tax credit or lower out-of-pocket costs for private insurance for those dependent family members who are eligible for coverage from a plan in the Marketplace or for Medicaid and CHIP coverage.

Understanding the Marketplace

With the implementation of the *Affordable Care Act*, every legal resident of the United States of America has the ability to shop for health insurance in their state's health insurance exchange. To be eligible for health insurance coverage through the marketplace, you must live in the United States, be lawfully present and not be in prison.

The Health Insurance Marketplace is sometimes known as the health insurance "exchange. Depending on the state you live in, the marketplace is run by either your state or the federal government. The marketplace is where you can find policies from health insurance companies which meet special criteria. It allows you to compare plans based on price, benefits, and other features. There has been a lot of controversy about the website where this information is found because of early technical difficulties.

The new health care law does not require you to purchase insurance through the marketplace. If you qualify for reduced costs, the price reductions or subsidies will only apply to certain plans within the marketplace. In general, the health insurance policies listed in the Marketplace only covers health care services provided by doctors, hospitals, and medical services within the United States.

Marketplace plans are listed in 4 different categories: bronze, silver, gold and platinum. Adults under 30 also have a 5th category: catastrophic. Catastrophic plans, only available to adults under 30, have very high deductibles and are designed only to protect from serious accident or extended illness. In rare cases, if a person qualifies for a **hardship exemption, they may also be able to purchase a catastrophic plan.**

CATASTROPHIC	less than **60%** of the total average costs of care
BRONZE	**60%** of the total average costs of care
SILVER	**70%** of the total average costs of care
GOLD	**80%** of the total average costs of care
PLATINUM	**90%** of the total average costs of care

Information on the marketplace website is written in plain language and designed to give you an easy way to compare premiums, benefits, and protections. The categories do not reflect the quality or amount of care the plans provide. Instead, the category reflects the amount of your monthly premium, co-payments, and total out of pocket costs. The maximum out-of-pocket costs for any plan listed in the Marketplace for 2014 are $6,350 for an individual and $12,700 for a family.

Health insurance plans listed in the Marketplace are offered by private insurance companies. In order to be listed in the marketplace, they need to offer the same core set of benefits called essential health benefits.

Types of Plans

Most health insurance plans offered in the Marketplace have networks of hospitals, doctors, specialists, pharmacies, and other health care providers. Networks include health care providers that the plan contracts with to take care of the plan's members. Depending on the type of policy you buy, care may be covered only when you get it from a network provider.

When comparing plans in the Marketplace, you will see a link to a list of providers in each plan's network. If staying with your current doctors is important to you, check to see if they are included before choosing a plan.

Health Maintenance Organizations (HMOs)

Typically HMOs and EPOs limit your health insurance coverage to providers to a specific list of doctors, hospitals, and other health care providers. This list is called a network. Different plans have different networks and providers

When you use a provider who is not listed in your network, you will probably be responsible for the entire costs of that service. When you purchase an HMO insurance policy, you are called a member. Members select a primary care doctor from within the network and require referrals to see a specialist.

Preferred Provider Organizations (PPOs) and Point-of-Service plans (POS)

With a PPO health insurance plan, you can receive health care services in or out of the network. If the health provider you use is outside of the network, you will pay more in services than if the provider you use is outside of the network. You can visit any doctor without a referral when you have a PPO health insurance plan.

High Deductible Health Plan (HDHP)

You will typically pay less for a high deductible health plan than other types of health insurance plans. In 2013, a HDHP will have a minimum deductible of $1250 for individual coverage and $2500 for family coverage.

When you have an HDHP, you can use a use health savings account to pay for qualified out of pocket medical costs. The amount you place in a health savings account can reduce the amount of taxes you pay.

Catastrophic Health Insurance Plan

A catastrophic health insurance plan covers essential health benefits with a very high deductible and like an HDHP, the premiums are often low compared to other plans. A catastrophic plan is designed to be a safety net only put into use in the event of a high medical cost event or illness. It only pays after you have paid thousands in medical bills.

Marketplace catastrophic plans allow you 3 annual primary care visits and preventive services with no fee. After you meet the larger deductible, they cover the same set of <u>essential health benefits</u> other plans offer. People with catastrophic plans are not eligible for lower monthly premiums or out-of-pocket costs.

Dental Coverage

Dental coverage is considered an essential health benefit for children under 18 years old. It is not considered essential for adults; therefore dental coverage may not be included in some of the marketplace plans.

After completing an application, you will be able to compare dental plans within the marketplace. If a plan within the marketplace includes dental coverage, it will not cost anything additional and you will only pay one premium for your health and dental benefits.

You may be offered a stand-alone dental plan. If you choose a stand-alone plan, you will pay a separate and additional premium for your dental coverage.

How to determine your income

If you are married and you will be completing a joint tax return, you will need to include the income of both you and your spouse. You will also need to include the income of any dependents who are required to file a tax return. Income includes wages, salaries, tips, unemployment compensation, social security payments and alimony.

If you are self-employed, you will include the net income from your business. You also need include any retirement, investment, pension, rental or other taxable income.

More information on how to report your income can be found in IRS Publication 525.

After you complete the application, your adjusted household income will be calculated for you. Your modified adjusted gross income (Magi) determines your eligibility for reduced health insurance costs. MAGI is usually your adjusted gross income plus any tax-exempt Social Security benefits (except for Supplemental Security Income (SSI), tax-exempt interest, and tax-exempt foreign income. This amount will be calculated for you when you complete an application.

How to Qualify

You do not need to qualify medically for any of these plans and they will cover your pre-existing medical conditions. In the past, health insurance companies could decide not to offer you coverage or charge you more for coverage because you have a medical condition. The laws changed in the 80's to keep large group insurance plans from excluding people based on health and now the law extends to all insurance plans.

Changing plans during open enrollment

After you select a plan within the marketplace, you still have time to change your mind. The soonest a plan will take effect is 15 days after you select coverage. No plan inside the marketplace will be effective prior to January 1, 2014.

During open enrollment, you'll need to select a health insurance plan by the 15th of the month in order for it to cover you by the 1st of the following month. You can change your mind about the plan you choose, but this will start your 15 day waiting period over again.

What if my current individual plan is changing or not being offered in 2014?

Starting 2014, most individual plans (not offered through an employer) must offer new benefits and protections. Some plans will be changed or replaced with plans that offer these protections. If this happens, you can choose to buy a plan in the Health Insurance Marketplace instead. If you switch to a Marketplace plan, you may qualify for lower costs based on your income.

Find out when your policy can end

Before you buy, you may want to find out when you can stop your policy--at any time, or only at the end of a plan or policy year. This could be useful to know if you'd like to switch to a Marketplace plan later.

If your plan ends outside open enrollment

If your individual plan ends outside the open enrollment period, you can still use the Marketplace to get a new plan. Because the plan is ending, you get a special enrollment period. You can select a plan listed in the Market 60 days before your individual plan ends. You can avoid a gap in coverage by selecting a plan by the 15th day the month before you need your new coverage to begin.

This special enrollment period only applies to people who's policy ends outside of the open enrollment period.

Minimum essential coverage

Qualified insurance plans need to offer minimum essential coverage. The following plans will all be considered qualified coverage:

- Any individual insurance plan you already have
- Any plan listed in the Marketplace
- Any employer based plan (including COBRA),

- Any retiree plans
- Medicare
- Medicaid
- The Children's Health Insurance Program (CHIP)
- TRICARE
- Veterans health care programs
- Peace Corps Volunteer plans

What if I don't purchase a health insurance plan?

By 2014 all non-exempt Americans will be covered by a health insurance plan, or face a tax penalty. If you already have health insurance, you do not need to make any changes. You do not need to have dental coverage to avoid the penalty.

If you can afford a health insurance policy but choose not to buy it, you will be subject to the **individual shared responsibility payment**. In 2014, the fee is the greater of 1% of your annual income or $95 per adult and $47.50 per child. The fee increases every year and by 2016 it is the greater of 2.5% of income or $695 per person whichever is higher.

The highest penalty for a family in 2014 is $285. You make the payment when you file your 2014 taxes, which are due in April 2015.

Sally and Joe have two children and make $50000 a year. They elect not to purchase health insurance in the year 2014. Sally and Joe's penalty would be the greater of $285 [($95x2) + ($47.50)] or $500 (1% of $50000.) Since the maximum fee in 2014 is $285, this is the only the only amount that will be payable in April of 2015.

Sally and Joe will be responsible for 100% of their medical care costs because they do not have health care insurance. After open enrollment ends on March 31, 2014, they won't be able to get health coverage through the Marketplace until the next annual enrollment period, unless they have a qualifying life event.

Exemptions from the penalty

There are exemptions for hardships, such as a man-made or natural disaster and other circumstances which would exempt you from paying the penalty if you do not have health insurance. People who are uninsured for less than 3 months of the year are exempt. If the lowest price health care plan available exceeds 8% of your household income, you may be exempt from the penalty.

Members of federally recognized tribes and recognized health care sharing ministries can be exempt from the fee. People serving a sentence in prison are also exempt from paying the fee.

If you have coverage from a job (or a family member's job), you're considered covered and won't have to pay the fee that uninsured people must pay.

You may be able to change to Marketplace coverage, but you might not qualify for lower costs on your premiums based on your income. This will depend on the type and cost of insurance the employer provides.

Hardship exemptions

There are some circumstances which would excuse you from the shared responsibility fee if they affect your ability to purchase a health insurance policy. You might qualify for this "hardship" exemption if you:

- Were homeless.
- Were evicted in the past 6 months
- Received a shut-off notice from a utility company.
- Were a recent victim of domestic violence.
- Experienced the death of a close family member.

- Had a substantial damage to your property from a fire, flood, or other disaster.
- You filed for bankruptcy in the last 6 months.
- You can't pay for medical expenses you incurred in the previous 2 years..
- You incurred unexpected expenses for a medically disadvantaged family member.
- Your state did not expand Medicaid eligibility but you would have qualified.

How to apply for an exemption

There are two ways to apply for an exemption (except for the religious belief or Indian Health Services exemptions) if you feel you qualify. First, you could claim the exemption on your tax return which is due April 15th of the following year. You can also apply for the exemption directly inside the marketplace. It is beneficial to attempt this because if you qualify for an exemption based on your employer-based plan being unaffordable, then you can purchase a catastrophic plan. The catastrophic plan covers less of your medical expense but is much lower in premium.

If you are trying to qualify for an exemption based on religious beliefs or Indian Health Services, you will need to fill out an exemption within the Marketplace. If you are not required to file taxes, you will not need to apply for an exemption even if you file a return to get a refund. If your gap of insurance coverage is less than 3 months, you will state such on your tax return and do not need to file for an exemption.

Certain Policies Will Not Avoid The Penalty

If your health insurance plan does not meet the minimum essential coverage, it will not qualify as coverage in 2014. Examples of policies which do not meet the minimum essential coverage are vision care or dental care exclusive plans, workers' compensation, cancer policies and plans which only offer discounts on medical services.

What about my current benefits from work?

If you have coverage from a job (or a family member's job), you're considered covered and will not be assessed a fine. **If you have insurance through your workplace or a family member's workplace you can elect to switch to a marketplace plan, but you may not** qualify for subsidies which reduce your marketplace premiums. In order to qualify for a subsidy, the job based plan's premium must be considered unaffordable or the plan must not meet minimum requirements. You also may lose any contributions your employer makes to your premiums.

Many employers share the cost of health insurance with their employees by paying a portion of the health insurance premium. Employers do not contribute to marketplace plans, therefore selecting a marketplace plan could cost considerably more than you pay through your employer.

So if Sally gets insurance through her husband's work she can keep the coverage for as long as it is offered. If Sally decides she wants to switch to the marketplace coverage because her husband's plan does not offer maternity benefits, she can, but she needs to keep in mind that her husband's employer pays $200 of her current plan's monthly premium and will not contribute this amount to the market place plans.

Sally may qualify for a subsidy to reduce her marketplace premium because her husband's plan does not offer the minimum essential coverage. (Maternity benefits are listed here) Sally, however, is Not Required to switch to a marketplace plan in order to avoid the penalty.

Any employment-based health plan you have qualifies as minimum essential coverage in order to have the penalty waived. You don't need to change to a Marketplace plan in order to avoid it because if you have a plan through work, you are considered covered.

Employer based plans Qualify

Any job-based health plan you currently have qualifies as <u>minimum essential coverage.</u> You don't need to change to a Marketplace plan in order to avoid the <u>penalty</u> that uninsured people have to pay starting in 2014.

If you'd like to explore Marketplace coverage options you can, but there are some important things to consider.

If your employer doesn't offer health insurance to part-timers

Part-time workers might qualify for lower costs on monthly premiums or out of pockets. Qualifications are based on income and household size. These savings are only given on select plans within the marketplace.

Part-timers may also qualify for Medicaid or Children's Health Insurance Program. When you apply for coverage through the Marketplace, you will be screened for eligibility in these programs.

If your employer does offer coverage

If you're offered coverage through an employer, you may buy insurance through the Marketplace instead. But in most cases you won't be able to get lower costs based on your income.

You would be eligible for lower costs only if the coverage your employer offers isn't considered <u>affordable</u> to you or doesn't meet certain <u>minimum standards</u>.

You can find out if your employer's coverage is affordable and meets minimum standards by completing an Employer Coverage Tool.

Losing employer-based coverage

If you become unemployed and lose your health insurance coverage, you have 2 options to replace the coverage: you can purchase a plan listed in the Marketplace or purchase COBRA for a limited amount of time.

The marketplace has an open enrollment period of October 1 through March 31st. Normally, your ability to purchase a plan through the marketplace is limited to that time period. If you lose the coverage you have through your employer however, you may purchase a plan outside of the open enrollment period.

Your other option is to purchase COBRA coverage. In most cases, a COBRA Plan can only be in effective for 18 months or less. People who's employer has paid a portion of the premium are often stunned by the high price of COBRA and when you purchase a COBRA plan, you do not qualify an individual to subsidies available within the marketplace.

A COBRA plan is a continuation coverage. When you have COBRA coverage, you usually have to pay the entire premium yourself, plus a small administrative fee. After you leave your job your former employer no longer pays for any of your insurance costs.

If you are self-employed with no employees, you are not considered an employer and you can use the individual Marketplace to find coverage that fits your needs.

Comparing employer and Marketplace plans

Many employers pay a part of the health insurance premiums offered to their employees. Employers do not pay any part of the health insurance premiums on plans within the Marketplace

An FSA is available only with job-based plans.

A Flexible Spending Account (FSA) is a special account which can be used to pay for **copayments**, **prescription drug**s, and other health care costs. You can put upto $2500 into an FSA accounts per year. Money you put into an FSA account is not taxable.

What if I have Medicare?

Medicare recipients are considered covered and do not need to make any changes to avoid the no health insurance penalty. Medicare and Medicare supplements (Medigap) are not available in the marketplace.

More people qualify for Medicaid beginning 2014

Many states are expanding their Medicaid programs to cover people at higher income levels. If your state is expanding Medicaid, it is likely you will qualify if you make less than $16000. If your income is higher, you may be able to buy a private insurance plan in the Health Insurance Marketplace and still be eligible for lower costs on monthly premiums and out-of-pocket costs based on your family size and income.

By applying through the new, single Marketplace application, you'll find out whether you're eligible for Medicaid or a private insurance plan at the same time.

Even if your state is not expanding Medicaid, you should apply for coverage to see if you qualify. Every state has existing coverage options that could work for you especially if you have children, are pregnant, or have a disability. Your qualification depends on income and family size. If eligible, you can receive free or low-cost care.

If you have retiree health benefits
If you receive retiree health benefits, you're considered covered under the health care law. You don't have to pay the fee some people without insurance must pay.
If you want to consider Marketplace insurance instead, you can. If you are not enrolled in retiree health coverage, you may qualify for lower costs on monthly premiums and out-of-pocket costs based on your household size and income. You'll find out whether you qualify.

If you want to find out if you qualify for lower costs on Marketplace coverage, you'll need to provide information about your household members and income.

CHIP Basics

CHIP is low-cost health insurance plan available to families that earn too much to qualify for Medicaid. CHIP policies can be applied for at any time of year.

What CHIP covers

The benefits covered through CHIP are different in each state, but all states provide comprehensive coverage, including:

- Routine check-ups
- Immunizations
- Doctor visits
- Prescriptions
- Dental and vision care
- Inpatient and outpatient hospital care
- Laboratory and X-ray services

- Emergency services

What CHIP costs

With CHIP coverage, many preventive healthcare services are provided free of charge. There are copayments for many others and there is usually a monthly premium required. The out of pocket costs for CHIP vary by state, however it should not exceed 5% of your household income.

How to qualify

Qualifications vary by state. You can find out if your family qualifies when you complete a Marketplace application. The CHIP agency will be notified of your application status if you qualify through the Marketplace.

Indian Health Services and Marketplace insurance

If you're an American Indian or an Alaska Native you may have new health insurance benefits and protections in the Marketplace.

Some benefits are available to members of federally recognized tribes. Others are available to people of

Indian descent or who are otherwise eligible for services from the Indian Health Service, tribal program, or urban Indian health program.

If you receive health care services from the Indian Health Service, tribal health programs, or urban Indian health programs, you can still elect to purchase coverage through the Marketplace.

Marketplace and Privacy

The Department of Health and Human Services and other federal agencies apply privacy and security standards which govern the use and transfer of information. No agency can require someone to provide citizenship status of someone who is not applying for coverage. Families with undocumented members cannot be denied coverage to those who are documented.

Social Security Numbers (SSNs) are required from any applicant or person receiving benefits.

Applicant information is verified though a data services hub. This hub lets the agency securely submit application information. The federal government returns data for the verification process.

Only questions which directly effect the eligibility of an applicant are asked in in the Marketplace application process.

Health insurance if you retire before age 65

If you retire before you're 65, you may use the <u>Health Insurance Marketplace</u> to buy a plan that meets your needs. Depending on your income and family size, you may be able to get l**ower costs on your monthly premiums** and . **When you apply** for coverage in the Marketplace, you'll also find out if you're eligible for **Medicaid.**

"Affordable" plans and the 9.5% standard

A job-based health plan is considered "affordable" if the employee's share of premiums for the lowest cost self-only coverage that meets the minimum value standard is less than 9.5% of their family's income. In other words, if your share of your premiums for a plan that covers only you (the employee)--not your family--is less than 9.5% of your family's income, the plan is considered affordable.

You may pay more than 9.5% of your income on premiums for spouse or family coverage from your employer. But affordability is determined only by the amount you'd pay for self-only coverage from your employer.

Modified adjusted gross income and household income

When you fill out the Marketplace application, your estimated household income will be calculated using the information you provide. Your household income determines your eligibility for lower costs on Marketplace coverage.

Your household income is your modified adjusted gross income (MAGI) (joint MAGI if you're married), plus the MAGI of your dependents who make enough money to have to file a tax return.

MAGI is generally your adjusted gross income plus any **tax-exempt** Social Security benefits (except for Supplemental Security Income (SSI), which is not counted), tax-exempt interest, and tax-exempt foreign income.

You don't have to figure out your household income or MAGI yourself when you fill out your application. It will be done for you with the income information you include on the application.

If your household files more than one tax return it is highly recommended that you call the marketplace before completing an application at **1-800-318-2596**. The line is available 24 hours a day, 7 days a week. TTY users should call 1-855-889-4325.

New rights, protections, and benefits

The health care law includes important new rights, strong consumer protections, and key benefits that apply to most employer-based insurance plans. It **does a lot to expand the average Americans health care rights.**

pre-existing health conditions

Beginning in 2014 insurance companies can't turn you down or charge you more because you are sick or have a health condition. This is a big change for many individuals who were denied health insurance benefits or charged very large premiums because of health insurance conditions such as high blood pressure and diabetes.

If you are currently paying for an individual health insurance plan (not employer based) that has been in existence on March 23, 2010 (whether or not you joined the plan), your plan has been grandfathered. Grandfathered plans do not need to cover pre-existing conditions.

Health insurance companies are now held accountable for rate increases.

Much like public utility companies, health insurance companies must now publicly justify any rate increase of 10%. Grandfathered individual policies do not need to justify rate increases.

Health insurance companies cannot cancel your policy because of honest mistakes

Prior to 2014, insurance companies could discontinue coverage, declare your policy invalid, and ask you to pay back any money they had already spent for your medical care if you made a mistake on your application. It's now illegal for them to cancel your coverage if you made an honest mistake or left out information that has little bearing on your health. These new protections apply to all health insurance plans, including those that are grandfathered. This does not mean that your plan can't be canceled if you use false information on purpose or fail to pay your premiums.

Parity protections for mental health services

In general, limits applied to mental health and substance abuse services can't be more restrictive than limits applied to medical and surgical services. (In the past, policies could place a much lower dollar amount on these benefits compared to other medical issues.) The kinds of limits covered by the parity protections include:

- Financial, like deductibles, copayments, coinsurance, and out-of-pocket limits
- Treatment, like limits to the number of days or visits covered

- Care management, like being required to get authorization of treatment before getting it

Mental and behavioral health

Marketplace plans can't deny you coverage or charge you more just because you have a pre-existing condition. This includes mental health and substance use disorder conditions.

Coverage for treatment of pre-existing conditions begins as soon as your Marketplace coverage is in effect. There's no waiting period for coverage of these services.

Essential Health Benefits

Essential health benefits are minimum requirements for all plans in the Marketplace. Every health insurance plan offered in the Marketplace will offer the same set of essential health benefits. These are services which all plans must cover.

Ambulatory patient services

Emergency services

Hospitalization

Maternity and newborn care

Mental health and substance use

Prescription drugs

Rehabilitative services

Laboratory services

Pediatric services

Preventive Services

Some plans may offer additional coverage. You can compare each plan side-by-side in the Marketplace.

Some rights and protections don't apply yet

No matter how you buy insurance before the Marketplace opens, be aware that some protections and benefits of the health care law are not yet in effect and may not apply to your coverage.

- You may be denied coverage, charged more, or have certain kinds of care limited or excluded if you have a pre-existing condition.
- Women may be charged more than men.

- Plans do not have to offer essential health benefits, so it's very important to find out what each plan covers and excludes.

- You won't be able to get lower costs based on your income, as you might be able to with a Marketplace plan.

Grandfathered plans

Grandfathered plans do not need to meet the qualifications of essential health benefits. Grandfathered status depends on when the plan was created not when you joined it. Your plan provider should tell you if your coverage is with a grandfathered plan.

Your rights, protections, and benefits

The health care law provides important new rights, strong consumer protections, and key benefits that apply to most job-based insurance plans.

Insurance companies must give you at least 30 days' notice before canceling your coverage for any reason. This gives you time to appeal the decision and find a new health insurance policy.

You have the right to choose a doctor

This does not mean that you may go to any doctor you wish. It only means you can have a choice within your health insurance provider's provider network. Under this protection, you can choose a network pediatrician as your child's primary doctor and you do not need a referral to visit an ob-gyn. Emergency visits will not require higher copayments or prior approval even if they are outside your plan's network. These protections do not apply to grandfathered plans.

Children can get insurance under their parent's plan until they are 26

This applies even if they are married, not living with their parents, in school or financially independent. Beginning in 2014 adults who are eligible to enroll in an employer's plan can also remain covered under a parent's plan. This protection does apply to grandfathered plans.

Preventive care must be provided for free
Medical tests and exams that are conducted to prevent disease such as mammograms, colonoscopies and annual checkups must be paid for by your insurance company without a deductible or co-payment. This protection does not apply to grandfathered plans.

No lifetime or annual limits on essential benefits
Beginning in 2014, health insurance companies can no longer limit lifetime coverage or have annual limits. This means that they can't set a limit on what they will spend on essential health benefits. In the past, companies tracked how much they paid out in health care costs over the entire life of an individual. Many companies limited the amount they would pay to 1 million and later, 3 million dollars. If someone suffered a loss that required ongoing care, the insurance company would no longer pay for their care after they reached the million dollars in a lifetime, even if the million dollars was spread out over 25 years.

Health insurance companies can still put a yearly dollar limit and a lifetime dollar limit on health care services not considered <u>essential health benefits.</u>

Mental and behavioral health services are essential health benefits

Psychotherapy and counseling for substance abuse, sometimes listed as substance use disorder is included as an essential health benefit. Specific benefits depend on the state you live in and the health plan you choose.

Health insurance policies must cover childbirth

Prior to 2014, health insurance companies could turn expectant parents (both male and female) down until the child was born. If you were uninsured and expecting, you could be turned down, charged a higher premium, or have benefits excluded. In Texas, for example, no individual (not employer based) policy had maternity coverage even if it was purchased before a pregnancy.

Preventive health services

Preventive care occurs when you are not sick. It is designed to help you stay healthy. All health insurance plans listed in the Marketplace must cover the following list of preventive services without charging you a <u>copayment</u> or <u>coinsurance</u>. These services are provided without charge even before you have met your annual deductible. They must be provided by a network provider to be covered without charge.

Abdominal Aortic Aneurysm one-time screening for men 65 to 75 who have ever smoked

Screenings for Alcohol Misuse, Depression, Blood Pressure and Obesity

Aspirin use for men ages 45 to 79 and women ages 55 to 79

Cholesterol, Colorectal Cancer and Diabetes (type 2) screening based on age and or risk.

Diet counseling for those at higher risk for chronic disease

HIV screening for adults ages 15 to 65, and others with increased risk

Immunization vaccines

Sexually Transmitted Infection, and Syphilis Screening for adults at higher risk

For Women:

Breast Cancer Genetic Test Counseling for women at high risk

Breast Cancer Chemoprevention Counseling for women at high risk

Mammography Screenings every 1 to 2 years

Clamydia Infection Screenings

Cervical Cancer Screening

FDA approved contraception (not required by health plans sponsored by exempt religious employers.

Domestic and Interpersonal Violence Screening and Counseling

Folic Acid

HPV screening every 3 years

Osteoporosis screening for women over age 60

For Pregnant Women:

Anemia screening

Breastfeeding comprehensive support and counseling

Gestational Diabetes Screening

Hepatitis B Screening

Rh Incompatibility screening

Urinary Tract infection screening

Health insurance plans must cover the cost of a breast pump. This can be in the form of a rental or a new one you can keep. The insurance provider can choose which type of pump they cover, how long they will rent one on your behalf and if you will receive it before or after you have the baby.

Covered contraceptive methods

All Food and Drug Administration-approved contraceptive methods prescribed by a woman's doctor are covered, including: Barrier methods ,Hormonal methods,Implanted devices, Emergency contraception, Sterilization procedures,Patient education and counseling

Preventive health services for children

All health insurance plans in the Marketplace and many other plans must cover the following preventive services for children without charging you a <u>copayment or coinsurance</u> even if you have not met your deductible.

The availability of the preventive service depends on the age, risk factors and location of the child.

Screenings for :

Autism,

blood pressure

cervical dysplasia

depression

hearing

hematocrit or hemoglobin

emoglobinoathies or sickle cell

HIV

Hyperthyroidism

Lead

Obesity

Oral Health Risk

PKU

Vision

Flouride and Iron Supplements

Behavior assessments, certain immunizations and height, weight, BMI measurements.

No matter what state you live in, you can use the Marketplace. Some states operate their own Marketplace. In other states, the Marketplace is run by the Federal government. Find the Health Insurance Marketplace in your state.

You have the right to appeal

If an insurance company refuses to pay a claim, they must tell you why. Under the new law, they also must tell you how you can dispute their decision. This law does not apply to <u>grandfathered plans</u>.

There are two ways you can make an appeal. If you believe the company made a mistake, you can request an internal appeal . If they still deny payment, you can request an external review.

An external review is done by an independent (outside the insurance company) organization. Depending on the state you live in, you may need to request several internal reviews before you are granted an external review.

What kinds of denials can be appealed?

You can file an internal appeal if your health plan won't provide or pay some or all of the cost for health care services you believe should be covered. The plan might issue a denial because:

- The benefit isn't offered under your health plan

- Your medical problem began before you joined the plan

- You received health services from a health provider or facility that isn't in your plan's approved network

- The requested service or treatment is "not medically necessary"

- The requested service or treatment is an "experimental" or "investigative" treatment

- You're no longer enrolled or eligible to be enrolled in the health plan

- It is revoking or canceling your coverage going back to the date you enrolled because the insurance company claims that you gave false or incomplete information when you applied for coverage

Internal Appeals

An internal appeal must be completed within 30 days if your appeal is for a pending healthcare service. If you have already received the treatment, the decision must me made withing 60 days. Your insurance company will provide you with decision in writing. If the final decision ends in a denial, you can request an external review.

If you are awaiting urgent care, you can file an expedited appeal. This means you can file an internal and external appeal at the same time if your life is in jeopardy. Your appeal must be answered within 4 days.

You must file your internal appeal within 180 days (6 months) of receiving notice that your claim was denied. If you have an urgent health situation, you can ask for an external review at the same time as your internal appeal.

External Review

Any denial of medical coverage that you or your provider disagree with can be submitted for an external review. You can also request an external review if the insurance company determines a treatment is experimental or if your coverag is canceled because they claim you gave false information when you applied for coverage.

To file an external review, you need to file a written request for an external review within 60 days. An external reviewer will issue a final decision: They will either uphold your insurer's decision or decide in your favor. By law, your insurer must accept the external reviewer's decision.

You can appoint a representative to file an external review on your behalf. An authorized representative form is available at:www.externalappeal.com

What to consider when choosing your plan

Balancing monthly premiums with out-of-pocket costs

When choosing a health insurance plan, you'll want to carefully consider both the monthly premium and the total out of pockets costs offered by the plans.

The premiums of lower out-of-pocket plans are typically higher than plans which pay less on your behalf. For example, in the marketplace, the Gold plan will cost you more per month, but you'll be responsible for less when you use the doctor or another medical service. A Bronze plan on the other hand will cost you less per month but you will pay more for your medical services.

Different types of health insurance plans meet different needs. When considering which Marketplace health insurance plan to buy you should ask yourself how often you visit the doctor or fill prescriptions. A Gold or Platinum plan will benefit you if you use these services often, if you don't, then you may benefit more from a Bronze or Silver plan. Keep in mind that the Bronze and Silver plan will also pay less if you are in an accident or have another unexpected claim.

If you are under 30 or qualify for a hardship, you may purchase the catastrophic plan which costs less per month, has a lower deductible, but has a greater out of pocket costs.

New options for the self-employed

If you are self-employed, you now have more health coverage options.

You can use the Marketplace to find health coverage that fits your budget and meets your needs. You can compare important features of several plans side-by-side, all of them offering a full package of essential health benefits. You can see what your premium, deductibles, and out-of-pocket costs will be before you decide to enroll. You can't be denied coverage or charged more because you have a pre-existing health condition.

If you currently have individual insurance--a plan you bought yourself, not the kind you get through an employer--you may be able to change to a Marketplace plan. Learn more about changing individual insurance plans.

How to know if you're "self-employed"

If you run an income-generating business with no employees, then you're considered self-employed (not an employer) and can get coverage through the Marketplace. You're not considered an employer even if you hire independent contractors to do some work. If you have employees (generally, workers whose income you report on a W-2 at the end of the year) you're considered an employer. Then you could get coverage for yourself and your employees through the SHOP Marketplace. Learn more about how to determine if you have employees.

Glossary

Accountable Care Organization (ACO): An umbrella of health care providers such as doctors and hospitals which provide coordinated coverage for Medicare patients. The purpose of this organization is to prevent unnecessary procedures through effective communication.

Adjusted Community Rating (ACR): Insurers selling personal or small group plans can adjust premiums based only on family size, place of residency, tobacco use and age. People in Nevada typically pay more for health insurance because of the higher medical needs in that state. New Jersey law forbids insurers from charging more because of tobacco.

Affordable: You are eligible for premium discounts in the Marketplace if your employer's coverage is not considered affordable. Your employer based health plan is considered if your share of the premium (for you not your family) is 9.5% of your income or less. Percentages are based on annual premiums and annual salaries In order for the coverage to be considered affordable, the lowest-cost coverage for the employee must be less than 9.5% of the employee's income.

Annual Limit: A cap on the amount an insurance company will pay in one year. Essential health benefits can no longer have an annual cap, however some other benefits may be limited.

Catastrophic Coverage: A catastrophic health plan only pays out after a very large deductible. These plans are designed to prevent a financial burden in the event of a large medical event. The plans usually have a very high deductible and provide less coverage than other types of plans. Within the marketplace, these policies are only available to adults under 30 and in rare occurrences, to others with hardship exemptions.

Deductible: The amount you pay before the health insurance company makes any payments for your healthcare. Many preventive healthcare costs are paid before you pay your deductible. Typically, the higher your deductible, the lower health insurance premium.

Employer Mandate: Beginning in 2015, employers with 50 or more employees are required to provide insurance for all full-time employees or pay a per-employee penalty.

Essential Health Benefits: 10 categories of healthcare which must be included by individual and small group health insurance plans. The categories are: hospitalization, lab services, rehabilitation, outpatient, emergency care, prescription drugs, maternity care, preventive services, mental health, and pediatric services. Care for children must also include oral and vision care. Under the new healthcare law, the benefits for these services cannot be capped. Individual coverage that does not include these benefits will not qualify you to avoid the tax penalty.

Exchanges: The are the locations also called the marketplace where you can apply for health insurance coverage, compare plans, and discover if you qualify for special discounts. Some states run their own exchange, others are listed by the Federal government.

Lifetime Benefit Maximum: The highest dollar amount an insurance company will pay for any one individual. The new healthcare law prevents lifetime caps from being placed on the 10 "essential health benefits."

Marketplaces: Online health insurance markets in each state where consumers can get private health insurance. Also, called exchanges.

Medicaid: A federal and state-funded insurance program for low-income individuals and families.

Medical Loss Ratio (MLR): The new healthcare law requires insurance companies to pay out at least 80% of the premiums they collect. If they pay less than 80% in medical claims, they must refund a portion of the premiums they have collected. This assures that you will not be overpaying premiums.

Minimum value

A healthcare plan is considered minimum value if it pays at least 60% of the total cost of your medical services.

Out-of-Pocket Maximum: The highest amount you will pay in medical costs in any given year. The Marketplace policy limits are $6,350 for an individual and $12,700 for a family.

Pre-existing Condition: A medical condition that you have had treatment for or continue to receive treatment for, such as high bloodpressue or diabetes. The new healthcare law prevents insurance companies from denying you coverage because of a preexisting.

Premium: The monthly payment you make to the insurance company.

Preventive Care Services: Medical services such as mammograms, and annual checkups that occur without being sick. Certain preventive care services are provided without a copayment or deductible.

Qualified Health Plan: Any insurance plan sold on the exchange must be certified by the state and federal government to show it meets minimum standards. Once certified, it becomes a qualified health plan.

Small-Business Health Care Tax Credit: Some businesses with less than 25 full-time employees whose salary is less than $50,000 will qualify for a tax credit for a portion of the premiums they pay on their employee's behalf.

Tax Penalty: Individuals who can afford health insurance but do not purchase it, will be subject to a fee. More information about the fee and qualifying exemptions is available in this guide.

www.ingramcontent.com/pod-product-compliance
Lightning Source LLC
Chambersburg PA
CBHW071801170526
45167CB00003B/1121